Baking with Fruit

Baking with Fruit

Delicious cakes, pastries and desserts

This edition published by Parragon Books Ltd in 2013
LOVE FOOD is an imprint of Parragon Books Ltd

Parragon Books Ltd
Chartist House
15–17 Trim Street
Bath, BA1 1HA, UK
www.parragon.com/lovefood

ISBN 978-1-4723-2973-8

Printed in China

Recipes, photographs and food styling: Patrik Jaros / www.food-experts-group.com
Edited by: Sabine Vonderstein & Patrik Jaros
Lace: from the book 'Lace', published by The Pepin Press, www.pepinpress.com

Notes for the Reader
This book uses both metric and imperial measurements. Follow the same units of measurement throughout; do not mix metric and imperial. All spoon measurements are level: teaspoons are assumed to be 5 ml, and tablespoons are assumed to be 15 ml. Unless otherwise stated, milk is assumed to be full fat and eggs are medium.

Garnishes, decorations and serving suggestions are all optional and not necessarily included in the recipe ingredients or method.

The times given are an approximate guide only. Preparation times differ according to the techniques used by different people and the cooking times may also vary from those given. Optional ingredients, variations or serving suggestions have not been included in the time calculations.

Recipes using raw or very lightly cooked eggs should be avoided by infants, the elderly, pregnant women, convalescents and anyone suffering from an illness. Pregnant and breastfeeding women are advised to avoid eating peanuts and peanut products. Sufferers from nut allergies should be aware that some of the ready-made ingredients used in the recipes in this book may contain nuts. Always check the packaging before use.

Contents

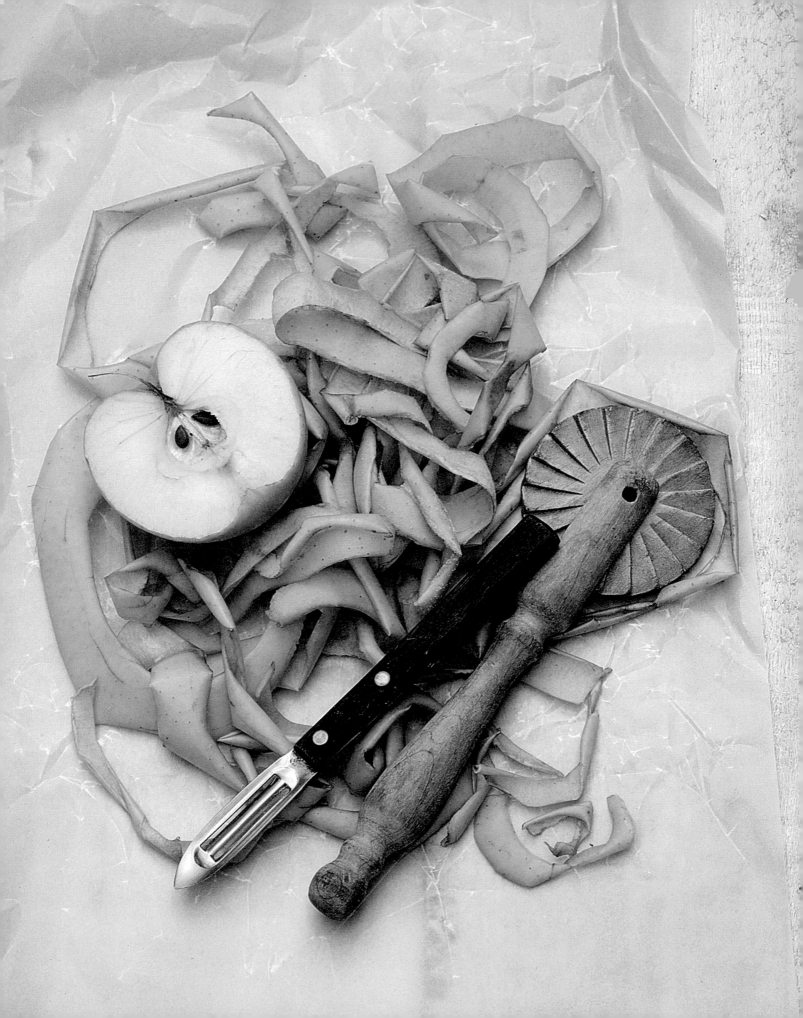

Foreword

Fresh, sweet and juicy fruit of almost every variety can be used in tempting baked treats of all shapes and forms. Family cakes, flans, tarts, pastries, desserts and traybakes can all incorporate the sensory pleasures of fruit from the garden or the market. Nowadays most kinds of fruit are available to be enjoyed all year round, but it makes sense to pay attention to the seasons when choosing which cake to bake. Rhubarb, for example, is only available in the spring, while plums taste best when they are at their ripest in late summer.

The authors have reinterpreted traditional and well-known recipes as well as creating some exciting new flavour combinations, to produce a collection of over 40 delicious cakes and bakes using fresh fruit. From delectable little tartlets to refreshing fruit flans, this book provides a wealth of ideas to inspire. Whether it's for a cosy afternoon get-together over tea and cakes, a Sunday visit by relatives or a fun-packed children's birthday – there's a fruity treat to suit every taste and every occasion.

Let yourself be tempted by classics such as Grandma's Cherry Cake or Lemon Sponge Roll, unusual combinations such as Pomegranate Cheesecake or Fig and Orange Liqueur Cake, or modern creations such as Banana and Chocolate Flan or Chilled Buttermilk and Kiwi Fruit Flan. There are gorgeous photographs of all the cakes to entice you into having a go at making them, while also giving you some presentation ideas. Don't be discouraged if not every cake you bake turns out looking just like the picture first time – at least you can be sure it will taste good.

Happy baking!

Fruit for every season ...

Rhubarb Cake

Makes 1 cake 30 × 40 cm/
  12 × 16 inches

Preparation time: 45 minutes
Cooking time: 45 minutes

Cake
2 tbsp dried breadcrumbs
400 g/14 oz plain flour
2 tsp baking powder
250 g/9 oz butter, plus extra for
  greasing
125 g/4½ oz caster sugar
4 eggs
pinch of salt
100 ml/3½ fl oz milk

Topping
800 g/1 lb 12 oz rhubarb, trimmed
50 g/1¾ oz caster sugar
1 tsp vanilla sugar
icing sugar, for dusting

1 Preheat the oven to 180°C/350°F/Gas Mark 4. Grease a 30 x 40-cm/12 x 16-inch baking tray and sprinkle with the breadcrumbs.

2 To make the cake, sift together the flour and baking powder. Put the butter into a large bowl and beat with an electric mixer until fluffy, then gradually add the sugar, eggs, salt and flour mixture, beating after each addition until combined.

3 Add the milk, a little at a time, beating until smooth. Spoon the mixture into the prepared tray and level the surface with a palette knife.

4 To make the topping, cut the rhubarb into 2-cm/¾-inch lengths. Mix with the caster sugar and vanilla sugar.

5 Spread the rhubarb pieces evenly over the mixture. Bake in the preheated oven for about 45 minutes. Remove from the oven, leave to cool and dust with icing sugar before serving. Best served lukewarm with whipped cream or vanilla ice cream.

Tip: To make vanilla sugar, cut a vanilla bean into 4 pieces and pop the pieces into a jar of caster sugar and set aside for 2–3 weeks, or until needed.

Strawberry and Lemon Tart

Makes 1 tart 28 cm/11 inches

Preparation time: 55 minutes, plus
  30 minutes to chill
Cooking time: 1 hour 10 minutes

Pastry
*175 g/6 oz plain flour, plus extra
  for dusting*
1 egg
75 g/2¾ oz butter
30 g/1 oz caster sugar
pinch of salt

Filling
200 ml/7 fl oz milk
200 ml/7 fl oz whipping cream
25 g/1 oz icing sugar
grated rind of 2 lemons
4 egg yolks

Topping
100 g/3½ oz blackcurrants
50 g/1¾ oz icing sugar
600 g/1 lb 5 oz ripe strawberries
*grated rind of 1 small lemon,
  for sprinkling*

1 To make the pastry, mix together the flour, egg, butter, sugar and salt in a mixing bowl, then knead by hand until a smooth dough forms. Wrap the dough in clingfilm and chill in the refrigerator for at least 30 minutes.

2 Meanwhile, to make the filling, put the milk into a saucepan with the cream, icing sugar and lemon rind. Bring to the boil, remove from the heat, then leave to infuse for 30 minutes. Gently whisk the egg yolks into the lemon cream.

3 Preheat the oven to 180°C/350°F/Gas Mark 4. Line a 28-cm/ 11-inch round, fluted tart tin with baking paper.

4 Roll out the pastry on a work surface lightly dusted with flour to a 30-cm/12-inch round. Use to line the prepared tin, trimming off any excess with a sharp knife. Prick the base with a fork in several places.

5 Line the pastry with baking paper, then fill with baking beans and bake on the bottom shelf of the preheated oven for 15 minutes. Remove the paper and beans and bake for a further 15 minutes, then remove from the oven and reduce the oven temperature to 140°C/275°F/Gas Mark 1. Pour the warm egg mixture into the pastry case and return to the oven for about 40 minutes until set. Remove from the oven and leave to cool completely.

6 To make the topping, thoroughly mash the blackcurrants and mix them with the icing sugar, then pass the mixture through a fine sieve to make a purée.

7 Top the tart with a tightly packed layer of strawberries, then drizzle over the blackcurrant purée and sprinkle with lemon rind.

Strawberry Tartlets with Vanilla Crème

❧ ◆◆◆ ❧

Makes 4 tartlets

Preparation time: 40 minutes, plus
  30 minutes to chill
Cooking time: 18 minutes

Sponge
butter, for greasing
2 eggs, separated
85 g/3 oz caster sugar
1 tbsp vanilla sugar (see page 10)
pinch of salt
50 g/1¾ oz plain flour, plus extra
  for dusting
50 g/1¾ oz cornflour

Vanilla crème
2 eggs, separated
1 sachet vanilla blancmange
  powder
350 ml/12 fl oz milk
150 ml/5 fl oz whipping cream
85 g/3 oz caster sugar
1 tsp vanilla sugar

Topping
2 tbsp flaked almonds
icing sugar, for toasting and dusting
600 g/1 lb 5 oz strawberries

1 Preheat the oven to 200°C/400°F/Gas Mark 6. Grease four 10-cm/4-inch round tartlet tins and dust with flour.

2 To make the sponge, put the egg yolks into a bowl and beat with an electric mixer until fluffy, adding the caster sugar and vanilla sugar a little at a time. In a separate bowl, whisk the egg whites with the salt until they hold stiff peaks. Mix the flour with the cornflour and fold into the egg yolk mixture with the egg whites.

3 Divide the mixture among the prepared tins and level the surface with a palette knife. Bake on the bottom shelf of the preheated oven for about 18 minutes until golden yellow. Leave to cool slightly, then turn out onto a wire rack to cool completely.

4 To make the vanilla crème, blend the egg yolks with the blancmange powder and 4 tablespoons of the milk. Put the remaining milk into a saucepan, add the cream, caster sugar and vanilla sugar and bring to the boil. Pour in the blancmange mixture and bring to the boil, stirring constantly, then remove from the heat. Pour the crème into a bowl, cover with clingfilm and chill in the refrigerator for 30 minutes. Remove from the refrigerator and whisk vigorously with a balloon whisk.

5 To make the topping, toast the flaked almonds with a little icing sugar in a dry frying pan until golden brown.

6 Spread the vanilla crème on top of the sponge bases. Place the strawberries on top with their points facing upwards. Sprinkle the almonds over the tartlets and dust with icing sugar.

Tip: Also tastes great with any other berries of your choice.

Fruits of the Forest Cheesecake

Makes 1 cake 24 cm/9½ inches

Preparation time: 20 minutes, plus
   4½ hours to chill

Base
250 g/9 oz digestive biscuits
120 g/4¼ oz butter
85 g/3 oz caster sugar
pinch of ground cinnamon

Topping
3 egg yolks
100 g/3½ oz caster sugar
500 g/1 lb 2 oz mascarpone cheese
500 g/1 lb 2 oz mixed berries,
   such as raspberries, blackberries
   and blueberries
12 sheets leaf gelatine
250 ml/9 fl oz whipping cream
85 g/3 oz sweet square biscuits
icing sugar, for dusting

1 To make the base, put the biscuits into a polythene bag and crush with a rolling pin until reduced to fine crumbs. Melt the butter in a saucepan, add the biscuit crumbs, sugar and cinnamon and mix to combine. Line the base of a 24-cm/9½-inch round springform tin with baking paper, press the biscuit mixture into the base, then chill in the refrigerator for 30 minutes.

2 To make the topping, put the egg yolks into a large bowl with the sugar and beat with an electric mixer until fluffy. Add the mascarpone cheese and 300 g/10½ oz of the berries. Soak the gelatine in cold water for 10 minutes, then squeeze out the water. Put the gelatine into a saucepan with a little water and heat over a low heat, stirring constantly, until dissolved. Stir the gelatine into the mascarpone mixture.

3 Whip the cream until it holds stiff peaks and fold it into the mascarpone mixture. Spread the mixture on the base, cover with clingfilm and chill in the refrigerator for 4 hours.

4 Remove the cake from the refrigerator and decorate with the remaining berries. Unclip and release the springform, arrange the biscuits around the edge of the cake and dust with icing sugar.

Mini Charlotte Russes

Makes 8 mini charlottes

Preparation time: 40 minutes, plus
  2 hours to chill
Cooking time: 12 minutes

Crème
5 sheets leaf gelatine
½ vanilla pod
200 ml/7 fl oz milk
60 g/2¼ oz white chocolate, broken
  into small pieces
3 egg yolks
40 g/1½ oz caster sugar
250 ml/9 fl oz whipping cream

Sponge fingers
3 eggs, separated
40 g/1½ oz icing sugar
1 tsp vanilla sugar (see page 10)
pinch of salt
50 g/1¾ oz caster sugar, plus extra
  for sprinkling
60 g/2¼ oz plain flour, sifted
30 g/1 oz cornflour

To decorate
150 g/5½ oz raspberries
150 g/5½ oz blueberries
icing sugar, for dusting

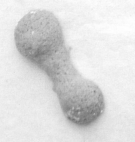

1 To make the crème, soak the gelatine in cold water for 10 minutes. Meanwhile, halve the vanilla pod lengthways and scrape out the seeds. Put the milk into a small saucepan, add the vanilla seeds and bring to the boil. Add the chocolate and leave to melt.

2 Put the egg yolks and caster sugar into a heatproof bowl and beat with an electric mixer until fluffy, then slowly stir in the hot milk. Set the bowl over a saucepan of gently simmering water and beat the crème until it thickens. Remove from the heat. Squeeze the water out of the gelatine, add the gelatine to the mixture and stir to dissolve. Pass through a fine sieve into a bowl. Transfer to the refrigerator to cool.

3 Whip the cream until it holds stiff peaks. Fold half the cream into the crème, then beat in the remainder with a balloon whisk. Divide the mixture between 8 high-sided 100-ml/3½-fl oz moulds, cover with clingfilm and chill in the refrigerator for 2 hours until set.

4 Preheat the oven to 180°C/350°F/Gas Mark 4. Line a baking sheet with baking paper. To make the sponge fingers, put the egg yolks into a bowl with the icing sugar and vanilla sugar and beat until fluffy. Whisk the egg whites with the salt and caster sugar until they hold stiff peaks. Fold the egg whites into the egg yolk mixture, then fold in the flour and cornflour.

5 Place the mixture in a piping bag fitted with a 1-cm/½-inch tip, and pipe the mixture onto the prepared baking sheet in 5-cm/2-inch lengths. Sprinkle with caster sugar and bake in the preheated oven for about 12 minutes. Remove from the oven and leave to cool.

6 Loosen the edges of the charlottes with a knife and turn them out of the moulds. Arrange the sponge fingers around the edges, decorate the tops with the fruit, dust with icing sugar and serve.

Berry and Sparkling Wine Jelly with Crème Fraîche

Makes 1 jelly 600 ml/1 pint

Preparation time: 25 minutes,
  plus 6 hours to set

12 sheets leaf gelatine
700 ml/1¼ pints dry white sparkling
  wine
60 g/2¼ oz caster sugar
1 tsp vanilla sugar (see page 10)
200 g/7 oz strawberries, halved
150 g/5½ oz blackberries
150 g/5½ oz blackcurrants
150 g/5½ oz raspberries
125 g/4½ oz blueberries
250 ml/9 fl oz crème fraîche
1 tsp icing sugar

1 Soak the gelatine in cold water for about 10 minutes.

2 Meanwhile, put 100 ml/3½ fl oz of the wine into a saucepan with the caster sugar and vanilla sugar and heat over a low heat. Squeeze out the gelatine and add it to the wine, stirring to dissolve. Pour into a bowl and add the remaining wine. As soon as the jelly starts to set, add all the berries, then pour into a 600-m/1-pint glass mould. Cover with clingfilm and chill in the refrigerator for about 6 hours until set.

3 Dip the mould briefly into a bowl of warm water to loosen the jelly. Turn out the jelly onto a serving plate.

4 Just before serving, mix the crème fraîche with the icing sugar and drizzle over the jelly.

Berry Tartlets with Butter Crumble

Makes 6 tartlets

Preparation time: 25 minutes, plus 30 minutes to chill
Cooking time: 35 minutes

Pastry
150 g/5½ oz plain flour
1 tsp baking powder
100 g/3½ oz butter, plus extra for greasing
150 g/5½ oz caster sugar
1 tsp vanilla sugar (see page 10)
pinch of salt
1 egg

Crumble topping
100 g/3½ oz plain flour
50 g/1¾ oz ground almonds
100 g/3½ oz caster sugar
1 tsp vanilla sugar
100 g/3½ oz softened butter

Filling
250 g/9 oz raspberries
150 g/5½ oz blueberries
150 g/5½ oz blackberries
icing sugar, for dusting

1 Preheat the oven to 180°C/350°F/Gas Mark 4. Grease six 10-cm/4-inch round tartlet tins.

2 To make the pastry, sift together the flour and the baking powder in a mixing bowl. Cut the butter into small pieces, rub into the flour mixture then add the caster sugar, vanilla sugar, salt and egg, and knead until a firm dough forms. Roll the dough into a ball, wrap with clingfilm and chill in the refrigerator for about 30 minutes.

3 Divide the dough into 6 pieces and press 1 piece into each of the prepared tins. Bake in the preheated oven for 15 minutes, then remove from the oven and leave to cool in the tins. Do not switch off the oven.

4 To make the crumble topping, put all the ingredients into a bowl and rub together with your fingertips until a crumbly texture is achieved.

5 To make the filling, scatter the berries over the pastry cases and sprinkle with the crumble topping.

6 Bake the tartlets in the oven for 20 minutes, then leave to cool in the tins. Release them from the tins using the point of a knife, dust with icing sugar and serve.

Blueberry Crumble with Walnuts

Makes 1 crumble 26 cm/10½ inches

Preparation time: 30 minutes, plus
   30 minutes to chill
Cooking time: 35 minutes

Base
*250 g/9 oz plain flour, plus extra
   for dusting
1 tsp baking powder
75 g/2¾ oz caster sugar
1 tsp vanilla sugar (see page 10)
125 g/4½ oz butter, plus extra for
   greasing
2 eggs
2 tbsp dried breadcrumbs*

Filling
*400 g/14 oz blueberries
2 egg yolks
90 g/3¼ oz caster sugar
1 tbsp vanilla sugar
3 tbsp milk
100 g/3½ oz ground walnuts
120 g/4¼ oz plain flour
icing sugar, for dusting*

1 To make the base, mix together the flour, baking powder, caster sugar and vanilla sugar. Cut the butter into small pieces, rub into the flour mixture, then add the eggs. Quickly knead the mixture until a smooth dough forms. Wrap in clingfilm and chill in the refrigerator for at least 30 minutes.

2 Preheat the oven to 160°C/325°F/Gas Mark 3. Grease a 26-cm/10½-inch round tart tin.

3 Roll out the dough, on a work surface lightly dusted with flour, into a round slightly larger than the prepared tin. Use it to line the tin, turning up the edge of the dough. Prick the base several times with a fork and scatter over the breadcrumbs.

4 To make the filling, spread the blueberries over the base. Mix the egg yolks with the caster sugar, vanilla sugar and milk. Add the walnuts and flour and rub together with your fingertips until a crumbly texture is achieved. Scatter the crumble mixture over the blueberries.

5 Bake in the preheated oven for about 35 minutes until the crumble is light brown. Leave to cool slightly, then dust with icing sugar just before serving.

Walnut Sponge Roll with Pear Filling

Makes 1 roll 40 cm/16 inches

Preparation time: 45 minutes,
   plus 5 hours to cool
Cooking time: 20 minutes

Sponge
4 eggs
4 tbsp lukewarm water
50 g/1¾ oz caster sugar
75 g/2¾ oz plain flour
45 g/1½ oz cornflour
50 g/1¾ oz ground walnuts
1 tsp baking powder

Filling
800 g/1 lb 12 oz pears
400 ml/14 fl oz pear juice
juice of ½ lemon
pinch of ground cinnamon
80 g/2¾ oz caster sugar
4 sheets leaf gelatine
250 ml/9 fl oz whipping cream
icing sugar, for dusting

1 Preheat the oven to 160°C/325°F/Gas Mark 3. Line a 30 x 40-cm/ 12 x 16-inch baking tray with baking paper.

2 To make the sponge, separate the eggs. Put the egg whites into a bowl with the water and whisk with an electric mixer until they hold stiff peaks. Slowly stir in the sugar, then carefully fold in the egg yolks. Mix together the flour, cornflour, walnuts and baking powder in a separate bowl, then carefully fold the flour mixture into the egg mixture.

3 Spread the mixture evenly in the prepared tin and bake in the middle of the preheated oven for about 20 minutes.

4 Remove from the oven and invert the tin onto a damp tea towel. Brush the baking paper with cold water and quickly peel it off the sponge. Use the tea towel to roll up the sponge from the long side, then leave to cool for 2 hours.

5 To make the filling, peel, core and slice the pears. Place the pear slices in a saucepan with the pear juice, lemon juice, cinnamon and sugar, bring to the boil, then remove from the heat. Soak the gelatine leaves in a little water, then squeeze out the water and stir the gelatine into the warm pear syrup until dissolved and leave to cool.

6 Whip the cream until it holds stiff peaks. As soon as the pear mixture starts to set, gently fold in the cream.

7 Carefully unroll the sponge and spread the filling over it. Roll up again immediately and leave to firm up for a further 3 hours. Dust with icing sugar just before serving.

Pear and Blackberry Cake

Makes 1 cake 30 × 40 cm/
  12 × 16 inches

Preparation time: 1 hour 15
  minutes, plus 1 hour to rise
Cooking time: 30 minutes

Cake
500 g/1 lb 2 oz plain flour, plus
  extra for dusting
50 g/1¾ oz caster sugar
pinch of salt
3 tsp easy-blend dried yeast (1½ x
  7g sachets)
125 g/4½ oz butter, plus extra for
  greasing
280 ml/9½ fl oz lukewarm milk

Topping
3 pears
rind of 1 orange
250 g/9 oz blackberries
50 g/1¾ oz soft light brown sugar
100 g/3½ oz quince jelly
icing sugar, for dusting

1 To make the cake, sift the flour, sugar and salt into a large bowl then stir in the yeast. Make a well in the centre.

2 Melt the butter in a saucepan over a low heat, then add to the dry ingredients with the milk, mixing to a soft, smooth dough. Cover with a damp tea towel and leave to rise in a warm place for about 30 minutes, or until risen and springy to the touch.

3 To make the topping, peel, quarter and core the pears, then cut the quarters into slices. Cut the orange rind into narrow strips.

4 Grease a 30 x 40-cm/12 x16-inch baking tray. Roll out the dough, on a work surface lightly dusted with flour, to a rectangle the size of the prepared tray. Lay the dough in the tray. Arrange the pears, blackberries and strips of orange rind evenly on top, pressing them into the dough slightly, then sprinkle over the brown sugar. Leave to rise for 30 minutes.

5 Meanwhile, preheat the oven to 200°C/400°F/Gas Mark 6.

6 Bake the cake in the preheated oven for about 30 minutes. Put the quince jelly into a small saucepan and heat over a low heat. Brush the jelly on the warm cake and leave to cool. Dust with icing sugar just before serving.

Blackberry and Semolina Cake

Makes 1 cake 22 cm/8½ inches

Preparation time: 30 minutes
Cooking time: 1 hour

Cake
100 g/3½ oz butter
160 g/5¾ oz caster sugar
3 eggs
grated rind and juice of 1 orange
100 g/3½ oz soft-wheat semolina
1 tsp baking powder
1 sachet vanilla blancmange
   powder
500 g/1 lb 2 oz low-fat curd cheese
   or quark

Topping
500 g/1 lb 2 oz blackberries
60 g/2¼ oz icing sugar, plus extra
   for dusting

1 Preheat the oven to 180°C/350°F/Gas Mark 4. Line a 22-cm/8½-inch round springform tin with baking paper.

2 To make the cake, put the butter into a bowl and beat with an electric mixer until fluffy. Add the sugar, eggs and orange rind and juice and beat until smooth.

3 Mix the semolina with the baking powder and blancmange powder. Stir into the butter mixture, then add the curd cheese and mix to combine.

4 Spoon the mixture into the prepared tin and level the surface. Bake in the preheated oven for about 60 minutes until golden brown.

5 Leave the cake to cool in the tin for 1–2 minutes, then unclip and release the springform and transfer the cake to a wire rack. Peel off the baking paper and leave the cake to cool completely.

6 To make the topping, crush 150 g/5½ oz of the blackberries with the icing sugar and pass through a fine sieve. Heap the remaining blackberries on top of the cake, pour over the sieved blackberries and dust with icing sugar just before serving.

Tip: The cake can also be made with fine polenta (instead of the semolina), which gives it a lovely yellow colour. Wild strawberries or blueberries can also be used for the topping.

Meringue and Puff Pastry Slices with Berries

Makes 8 slices

Preparation time: 30 minutes
Cooking time: 15 minutes

500 g/1 lb 2 oz ready-rolled puff
pastry (6 sheets)
plain flour, for dusting
1 egg yolk, beaten
30 g/1 oz flaked almonds
200 ml/7 fl oz whipping cream
125 g/4½ oz caster sugar
1 vanilla pod
2 egg whites
125 g/4½ oz blueberries
200 g/7 oz redcurrants
125 g/4½ oz raspberries
icing sugar, for dusting

1 Preheat the oven to 190°C/375°F/Gas Mark 5. Line a 30 x 40-cm/12 x 16-inch baking tray with baking paper.

2 Divide the pastry into two piles, using three sheets in each, dust with flour and roll out to a thickness of about 1 cm/½ inch. Lay the pastry on the prepared tray.

3 Brush the two slabs of pastry with the beaten egg yolk. Sprinkle over the almonds and bake on the bottom shelf of the preheated oven for about 15 minutes until golden brown. Remove from the oven and leave to cool.

4 Whip the cream with 25 g/1 oz of the caster sugar until it holds stiff peaks. Cover and chill in the refrigerator until required. Halve the vanilla pod lengthways and scrape out the seeds. Whisk the egg whites until they hold soft peaks, whisk in the remaining sugar a little at a time, then add the vanilla seeds. Beat until the egg white is glossy and holds stiff peaks. Fold in the whipped cream.

5 Split each piece of pastry in half horizontally. Spread the bottom halves with half of the meringue mixture, scatter the berries on top, and spread the remaining meringue mixture on top of the berries. Top with the remaining pastry halves. Dust with icing sugar just before serving and cut each piece into 4 slices.

Tip: The puff pastry slices can also be filled with a vanilla crème (see p. 14), and other fruits can be used.

Lime and Raspberry Tart

Makes 1 tart 24 cm/9½ inches

Preparation time: 45 minutes,
    plus 1 hour to chill
Cooking time: 1 hour 5 minutes

Pastry
*175 g/6 oz plain flour, plus extra
    for dusting*
1 egg
75 g/2¾ oz butter
30 g/1 oz caster sugar
½ tsp salt

Filling
250 ml/9 fl oz milk
250 ml/9 fl oz whipping cream
120 g/4¼ oz icing sugar
rind of 2 limes, in long strips
6 egg yolks
600 g/1 lb 5 oz raspberries

Crème
250 g/9 oz mascarpone cheese
*80 g/2¾ oz icing sugar, plus extra
    for dusting*
grated rind and juice of 1 lime
*grated lime rind, to decorate
    (optional)*

1 To make the pastry, put the flour, egg, butter, sugar and salt into a food processor and process to a smooth dough. Shape into a ball, wrap in clingfilm and chill in the refrigerator for about 30 minutes.

2 To make the filling, put the milk, cream, sugar and lime rind into a saucepan and bring to the boil, then remove from the heat and leave to infuse for 30 minutes. Remove the lime rind from the cream mixture and carefully whisk in the egg yolks.

3 Line the base of a 24-cm/9½-inch round tart tin with baking paper. Roll out the pastry on a work surface lightly dusted with flour into a 30-cm/12-inch round. Place it in the prepared tin, pressing it into the side of the tin and trimming any excess. Prick the base with a fork in several places, dust with a little flour and chill for 30 minutes.

4 Preheat the oven to 180°C/350°F/Gas Mark 4. Line the pastry case with baking paper, fill with baking beans and bake on the bottom shelf of the preheated oven for 15 minutes. Remove the paper and beans and bake for a further 15 minutes. Remove from the oven and reduce the oven temperature to 140°C/275°F/Gas Mark 1. Heat the egg mixture briefly, then pour it into pastry case, reserving 2 tablespoons, and bake for 35 minutes. Remove from the oven and leave to cool.

5 Arrange the raspberries on top of the tart, reserving a few to decorate.

6 To make the crème, beat the mascarpone cheese with the reserved egg mixture, the icing sugar and the lime rind and juice until smooth. Pour into the middle of the tart, leaving a border around the edge where the raspberries are still visible. Decorate with the reserved raspberries, dust with icing sugar, sprinkle some grated lime rind on top, if using, and serve.

Redcurrant and Blueberry Tartlets with Meringue

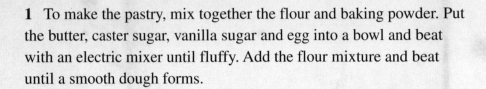

Makes 8 tartlets

Preparation time: 35 minutes
Cooking time: 25 minutes

Pastry
300 g/10½ oz plain flour, plus extra
   for dusting
1 tsp baking powder
200 g/7 oz butter, plus extra for
   greasing
100 g/3½ oz caster sugar
2 tsp vanilla sugar (see page 10)
1 egg

Filling
100 g/3½ oz blueberry jelly
250 g/9 oz blueberries
250 g/9 oz redcurrants

Meringue
3 egg whites
180 g/6 oz caster sugar
juice of ½ lemon

1 To make the pastry, mix together the flour and baking powder. Put the butter, caster sugar, vanilla sugar and egg into a bowl and beat with an electric mixer until fluffy. Add the flour mixture and beat until a smooth dough forms.

2 Preheat the oven to 180°C/350°F/Gas Mark 4. Grease eight 10-cm/4-inch tartlet tins and dust with a little flour.

3 Roll out the pastry on a work surface lightly dusted with flour to a thickness of 5 mm/¼ inch. Place the prepared tins close together and lay the pastry over the tops. Press into the tins and use a knife to trim the edges level with the top of the tins. Bake in the preheated oven for about 15 minutes, then remove from the oven and leave to cool. Do not switch off the oven.

4 To make the filling, stir the jelly until smooth and brush over the pastry cases. Gently mix together the blueberries and redcurrants and divide among the pastry cases.

5 To make the meringue, whisk the egg whites until they hold soft peaks, then add the sugar little by little. Whisk for a further 5 minutes on the highest speed setting until the egg whites are glossy and hold stiff peaks. Add the lemon juice and stir to combine. Transfer the meringue mixture to a piping bag fitted with a small tip and pipe dots of meringue onto the tartlets.

6 Bake in the oven for 10 minutes until the tips of the meringue are light brown. Remove from the oven and leave to cool before serving.

Gooseberry Meringue Cake

Makes 1 cake 26 cm/10½ inches

Preparation time: 40 minutes,
 plus approx 30 minutes to rise
Cooking time: 1 hour 5 minutes

Cake
*250 g/9 oz plain flour, plus extra
 for dusting*
60 g/2¼ oz caster sugar
pinch of salt
grated rind of lemon
*1 x 7 g sachet easy-blend dried
 yeast*
125 ml/4 fl oz lukewarm milk
1 egg, beaten
butter for greasing

Filling
*500 g/1 lb 2 oz low-fat curd cheese
 or quark*
20 g/¾ oz cornflour
120 g/4¼ oz caster sugar
1 tsp vanilla sugar (see page 10)
grated rind of 1 lemon
1 tbsp lemon juice
2 eggs
pinch of salt
*550 g/1 lb 4 oz red gooseberries,
 topped and tailed*

Meringue
3 egg whites
130 g/4¾ oz caster sugar

1 To make the cake, sift the flour, sugar, salt and lemon rind into a large bowl then stir in the yeast. Make a well in the centre.

2 Pour the milk and egg into the well in the dry ingredients and knead to a soft dough. Cover with a damp tea towel and leave to rise in a warm place for about 30 minutes, or until lightly risen and springy to the touch.

3 Meanwhile, to make the filling, put the curd cheese, cornflour, caster sugar, vanilla sugar, lemon rind, lemon juice, eggs and salt into a bowl and beat until smooth.

4 Preheat the oven to 180°C/350°F/Gas Mark 4. Grease a 26-cm/ 10½-inch round, 3-cm/1¼-inch deep, fluted tart tin with a loose base and place on a baking sheet.

5 Roll out the dough on a work surface lightly dusted with flour and use to line the base and sides of the prepared tin, pressing with your knuckles to fit the sides. Spread the cheese mixture over the base and level the surface, then scatter the gooseberries over the top, lightly pressing the fruit into the filling. Bake in the preheated oven for about 50 minutes.

6 Meanwhile, to make the meringue, whisk the egg whites in an electric mixer until they hold soft peaks, then add the sugar, a little at a time. Whisk for a further 5 minutes on the highest speed setting until the egg white is glossy and hold stiff peaks.

7 Remove the cake from the oven and spread the meringue on top, then return to the oven and bake for a further 15 minutes, until pale golden. Leave the cake to cool in the tin, then transfer to a cake plate to serve.

Plum and Puff Pastry Tart

Makes 1 tart 30 × 40 cm/
   12 × 16 inches

Preparation time: 30 minutes, plus
   15 minutes to chill
Cooking time: 35 minutes

Pastry
butter, for greasing
500 g/1 lb 2 oz ready-made
   puff pastry
plain flour, for dusting

Filling
350 g/12 oz plums
250 ml/9 fl oz crème fraîche
60 g/2¼ oz caster sugar
1 tsp vanilla sugar (see page 10)
pinch of ground cinnamon
3 eggs
1 tbsp cornflour
2 tbsp dried breadcrumbs
100 g/3½ oz plain chocolate

1 Grease a 30 x 40-cm/12 x 16-inch baking tray. Lay the pastry on a work surface, dust with flour and roll out the pastry to a rectangle slightly larger than the tray. Lay the pastry on the tray, turn up the edge and prick the base with a fork in several places. Chill in the refrigerator for about 15 minutes.

2 Meanwhile, to make the filling, halve and stone the plums. Put the crème fraîche, caster sugar, vanilla sugar, cinnamon, eggs and cornflour into a bowl and mix until smooth.

3 Preheat the oven to 190°C/375°F/Gas Mark 5.

4 Sprinkle the breadcrumbs over the pastry and cover with the filling mixture. Arrange the plums on top, lightly pressing them into the filling.

5 Bake the tart in the preheated oven for about 35 minutes until golden brown. Remove from the oven and leave to cool in the tray.

6 Put the chocolate into a heatproof bowl set over a saucepan of gently simmering water and heat until melted. Drizzle the chocolate over the tart with a fork. Cut the tart into pieces, arrange on a cake plate and serve.

Tip: This tart also tastes great made with apples, apricots or peaches, in season.

Mirabelle and Puff Pastry Tart

Makes 1 tart 24 cm/9½ inches

Preparation time: 30 minutes, plus
   15 minutes to chill
Cooking time: 35 minutes

Pastry case
butter, for greasing
250 g/9 oz ready-made puff pastry
plain flour, for dusting

Filling
400 g/14 oz mirabelle plums
250 ml/9 fl oz crème fraîche
100 g/3½ oz caster sugar
1 tsp vanilla sugar (see page 10)
3 eggs
1 tbsp cornflour
1 tbsp dried breadcrumbs
icing sugar, for dusting

1 Grease a 24-cm/9½-inch round tart tin. Lay the pastry on a work surface, dust with flour and roll out to a round slightly larger than the prepared tin. Lay the pastry in the tin, turn up the edge and prick the base with a fork in several places. Chill in the refrigerator for about 15 minutes.

2 Preheat the oven to 190°C/375°F/Gas Mark 5.

3 Meanwhile, to make the filling, stone the mirabelles. Put the crème fraîche, caster sugar, vanilla sugar, eggs and cornflour into a bowl and mix until smooth.

4 Scatter the breadcrumbs over the pastry case and cover with the filling mixture. Arrange the mirabelles on top, lightly pressing them into the filling.

5 Bake in the preheated oven for about 35 minutes until golden brown. Remove from the oven and leave to cool in the tin. Carefully remove the tart from the tin and transfer to a cake plate. Dust with icing sugar just before serving.

Tip: This cake also tastes great made with apples, apricots, peaches or plums, in season.

Bohemian Plum Strudel

Makes 1 strudel

Preparation time: 30 minutes, plus
   30 minutes to rest
Cooking time: 45 minutes

Pastry
130 ml/4¼ fl oz cold water
pinch of salt
1 tbsp sunflower oil, plus extra
   for brushing
1 egg yolk
250 g/9 oz plain flour, plus extra
   for dusting
melted butter, for greasing
fruit brandy such as plum brandy or
   Calvados, for drizzling
icing sugar, for dusting

Filling
400 g/14 oz plums
180 g/6¼ oz butter
100 g/3½ oz dried breadcrumbs
70 g/2½ oz ground almonds
150 g/5½ oz caster sugar
a pinch of ground cinnamon

1 To make the pastry, mix together the water, salt, oil and egg yolk in a mixing bowl. Add the flour and mix until smooth. Cover the dough and leave to rest for 30 minutes.

2 Turn out the pastry onto a tea towel lightly dusted with flour. Roll the pastry out as thinly as possible then, using the back of your hands, gently stretch it out. Brush with oil and a little melted butter, then drizzle with the brandy.

3 Preheat the oven to 180°C/350°F/Gas Mark 4. Grease a 30 x 40-cm/12 x 16-inch baking tray.

4 To make the filling, stone the plums, cut them into small slices and arrange on top of the pastry. Melt half the butter in a frying pan, add the breadcrumbs and sauté until brown. Mix with the almonds, caster sugar and cinnamon and scatter the mixture over the plums.

5 Use the tea towel to roll up the pastry and lay it in the prepared baking tray. Bake in the preheated oven for about 45 minutes. Meanwhile, melt the remaining butter and use to brush the strudel shortly before the end of cooking. Dust with icing sugar just before serving.

Breton Mirabelle Cake

Makes 1 cake 22 cm/8½ inches

Preparation time: 25 minutes
Cooking time: 45 minutes

butter, for greasing
250 g/9 oz mirabelle plums
3 eggs
75 g/2¾ oz caster sugar
pinch of salt
100 g/3½ oz plain flour
120 g/4¼ oz ground almonds
130 ml/4¼ fl oz whipping cream
icing sugar, for dusting

1 Preheat the oven to 180°C/350°F/Gas Mark 4. Grease a 22-cm/8½-inch high-sided fluted tart tin.

2 Carefully halve and stone the mirabelles, keeping the stalks in place if possible.

3 Put the eggs, sugar and salt into a bowl and beat with an electric mixer until fluffy. Add the flour, 1 tablespoon at a time, and beat to combine. Add the almonds, then gradually add the cream, continuing to beat until a thick, smooth dough forms.

4 Transfer the dough to the prepared tin. Arrange the 2 halves of each mirabelle together on top, stalk ends pointing upwards.

5 Bake in the preheated oven for about 45 minutes. Leave to cool, then remove from the tin. Dust with icing sugar just before serving.

Tip: Plums, apricots or blackberries can be used instead of mirabelles. Because it has a slightly sharp flavour, this cake tastes very good served with crème fraîche mixed with a little vanilla sugar.

Apricot and Rice Tart

Makes 1 tart 28 cm/11 inches

Preparation time: 45 minutes, plus
  30 minutes to chill
Cooking time: 50–60 minutes

Pastry
200 g/7 oz plain flour, plus extra
  for dusting
pinch of salt
100 g/3½ oz butter
1 egg
60 g/2¼ oz caster sugar

Filling
1 vanilla pod
750 ml/1⅓ pints milk
250 g/9 oz pudding rice
140 g/5 oz caster sugar
grated rind and juice of 1 lemon
1 cinnamon stick
500 g/1 lb 2 oz apricots
2 eggs, separated
pinch of salt
85 g/3 oz caster sugar
250 ml/9 fl oz crème fraîche
icing sugar, for dusting

1 To make the pastry, mix together the flour and salt on a work surface and make a well in the centre. Cut the butter into small pieces and place in the well, together with the egg and sugar. Knead until a smooth dough forms. Wrap in clingfilm and chill in the refrigerator for 30 minutes.

2 To make the filling, halve the vanilla pod lengthways and scrape out the seeds. Put the milk, rice, sugar, lemon rind and juice, cinnamon stick and vanilla pod and seeds into a saucepan and bring to the boil. Reduce the heat and simmer for about 20 minutes, stirring occasionally. Pour the mixture into a bowl, cover with clingfilm and leave to cool until lukewarm.

3 Preheat the oven to 180°C/350°F/Gas Mark 4. Line a 28-cm/ 11-inch tart tin with baking paper. Place the dough on a work surface lightly dusted with flour, divide into two pieces and press one piece over the base of the prepared tin. Roll the remaining piece into a sausage shape and press around the inner edge of the tin. Prick the base with a fork in several places.

4 Halve and stone the apricots. Whisk the egg whites with the salt until they hold stiff peaks, gradually adding 2 tablespoons of the sugar. Mix together the egg yolks, crème fraîche and the remaining sugar. Remove the cinnamon stick and vanilla pod from the rice. Mix the rice mixture with the egg mixture. Fold in the beaten egg whites.

5 Spread half the rice mixture in the pastry case, then arrange half the apricots on top. Spread the remaining rice on top, followed by the remaining apricots.

6 Bake in the preheated oven for 50–60 minutes. If it is browning too quickly, cover with foil. Dust with icing sugar before serving.

Apricot and Blueberry Cake

Makes 1 cake 30 × 40 cm/
  12 × 16 inches

Preparation time: 45 minutes
Cooking time: 40 minutes

Base
450 g/1 lb plain flour
200 g/7 oz caster sugar
50 g/1¾ oz vanilla sugar
  (see page 10)
200 g/7 oz butter, plus extra
  for greasing

Topping
150 g/5½ oz butter
125 g/4½ oz caster sugar
2 tsp vanilla sugar
2 eggs
500 g/1 lb 2 oz low-fat curd cheese
  or quark
grated rind of 1 lemon
2 tbsp lemon juice
1 sachet vanilla blancmange
  powder
750 g/1 lb 10 oz apricots
300 g/10½ oz blueberries
icing sugar, for dusting
whipping cream, to serve (optional)

1 Preheat the oven to 200°C/400°F/Gas Mark 6. Grease a 30 x 40-cm/12 x 16-inch baking tray.

2 To make the base, mix together the flour, caster sugar, vanilla sugar and butter in a mixing bowl. Cut the butter into small pieces and rub it in with your fingertips until a crumbly consistency is achieved. Spread two thirds of the crumble mixture over the base of the prepared tray, pressing down firmly. Bake in the preheated oven for about 10 minutes. Remove from the oven and reduce the oven temperature to 180°C/350°F/Gas Mark 4.

3 Meanwhile, to make the topping, put the butter, caster sugar and vanilla sugar into a bowl and beat with an electric mixer until fluffy. Add the eggs, one at a time, beating after each addition until creamy. Stir the curd cheese, lemon rind and juice, and blancmange powder into the mixture. Spread over the base.

4 Halve and stone the apricots. Arrange on top of the cream layer, alternating with the blueberries in diagonal stripes. Scatter the remaining crumble mixture on top of the fruit.

5 Bake the cake for 30 minutes. Leave to cool, then cut it into pieces, dust with icing sugar and serve with cream, if using.

Peach Tarte Tatin

Makes 1 tart 24 cm/9½ inches

Preparation time: 20 minutes
Cooking time: 15 minutes

1 kg/2 lb 4 oz peaches
85 g/3 oz butter
120 g/4¼ oz caster sugar
2 tsp vanilla sugar (see page 10)
500 g/1 lb 2 oz ready-made
 puff pastry
flour, for dusting
crème fraîche, to serve

1 Preheat the oven to 220°C/425°F/Gas Mark 7.

2 Halve and stone the peaches. Melt the butter in a saucepan. Sprinkle the base of a 24-cm/9½-inch ovenproof frying pan with the caster sugar. Arrange the peach halves on top in a tightly packed circle, cut edges facing downwards. Drizzle the melted butter evenly over the peaches, then sprinkle the vanilla sugar on top.

3 Place the pan over a medium heat to caramelize the sugar, tilting the pan slightly to keep the peach halves moving.

4 On a lightly floured surface, roll out the pastry into a 3-cm/1¼-inch-thick round slightly larger than the pan. Cover the peaches with the pastry, pressing down the edges and trimming any excess.

5 Bake in the middle of the preheated oven for about 15 minutes until golden brown. If the pastry starts to brown too quickly, cover it with foil.

6 Remove from the oven and turn out onto a plate. Serve warm with crème fraîche.

Soured Cream Cake with Nectarines

Makes 1 cake 26 cm/10½ inches

Preparation time: 30 minutes
Cooking time: 1 hour 5 minutes

butter, for greasing
40 g/1½ oz dried breadcrumbs
3 nectarines
750 g/1 lb 10 oz low-fat curd cheese
  or quark
100 ml/3½ fl oz soured cream
3 eggs
150 g/5½ oz caster sugar
1 sachet vanilla blancmange
  powder
100 ml/3½ fl oz sunflower oil
100 ml/3½ fl oz milk
50 g/1¾ oz ground almonds
icing sugar, for dusting

1 Preheat the oven to 160°C/325°F/Gas Mark 3. Grease a 26-cm/10½-inch round springform tin and sprinkle with the breadcrumbs.

2 Stone the nectarines, then cut them into thin slices.

3 Put the curd cheese into a mixing bowl with the soured cream, eggs, sugar, blancmange powder, oil, milk and almonds, and beat with an electric mixer until smooth and creamy.

4 Spoon the mixture into the prepared tin and arrange the nectarine slices in a circle on top. Bake in the preheated oven for about 1 hour 5 minutes.

5 Remove from the oven and leave to cool in the tin, then carefully turn out of the tin and transfer to a cake plate. Dust with icing sugar just before serving.

Cherry Marble Cake

Makes 1 cake 26 cm/10½ inches

Preparation time: 30 minutes
Cooking time: 1 hour

2 tbsp dried breadcrumbs
250 g/9 oz softened butter, plus
  extra for greasing
250 g/9 oz caster sugar
2 tsp vanilla sugar (see page 10)
4 eggs
500 g/1 lb 2 oz plain flour
2 tsp baking powder
½ tsp salt
100 ml/3½ fl oz milk
300 g/10½ oz cherries
30 g/1 oz cocoa powder
icing sugar, for dusting

1 Preheat the oven to 180°C/350°F/Gas Mark 4. Grease a 26-cm/10½-inch deep, fluted ring tin and sprinkle with the breadcrumbs.

2 Put the butter into a bowl and beat until creamy, gradually adding the caster sugar and vanilla sugar. Add the eggs, one at a time, beating after each addition until smooth.

3 Sift the flour with the baking powder and salt. Gradually add to the butter mixture, alternating with the milk, beating until the mixture is thick and smooth.

4 Spoon half the mixture into the prepared tin. Stone the cherries and scatter half of them over the cake mixture, pressing them in slightly. Stir the cocoa powder into the remaining mixture.

5 Spoon the cocoa mixture over the cherries, then scatter the remaining cherries on top. Using the handle of a wooden spoon, gently swirl the two layers together to produce a marbled effect.

6 Bake in the preheated oven for about 1 hour. Leave to cool in the tin for 5 minutes, then turn out onto a wire rack to cool completely. Transfer to a cake plate and dust with icing sugar just before serving.

Morello Cherry Clafoutis

Makes 1 clafoutis 28 cm/11 inches

Preparation time: 45 minutes, plus
  30 minutes to rest
Cooking time: 20 minutes

2 eggs, separated
60 g/2¼ oz caster sugar
1 tbsp vanilla sugar (see page 10)
100 g/3½ oz plain flour
200 ml/7 fl oz milk
pinch of salt
pinch of grated lemon rind
250 g/9 oz morello cherries
2 tbsp vegetable oil
icing sugar, for dusting
whipped cream, to serve (optional)

1 Put the egg yolks, caster sugar and vanilla sugar into a large bowl and beat with an electric mixer until fluffy. Add the flour, milk, salt and lemon rind and beat until smooth. Leave to rest for 30 minutes.

2 Preheat the oven to 180°C/350°F/Gas Mark 4. Stone the cherries.

3 Whisk the egg whites until they hold stiff peaks, then carefully fold them into the batter.

4 Heat the oil in a 28-cm/11-inch ovenproof frying pan. Pour in the batter and cook over a low heat for 5 minutes, until the underside is lightly browned. Scatter the cherries over the surface.

5 Transfer the pan to the preheated oven and bake for about 15 minutes. Slide the clafoutis out of the pan onto a cake plate. Dust with icing sugar and serve lukewarm with whipped cream, if using.

Grandma's Cherry Cake

Makes 1 cake 20 × 30 cm/
  8 × 12 inches

Preparation time: 25 minutes
Cooking time: 1 hour

2 tbsp dried breadcrumbs
500 g/1 lb 2 oz cherries
150 g/5½ oz softened butter,
  plus extra for greasing
150 g/5½ oz caster sugar
4 eggs, separated
70 g/2½ oz ground almonds
150 g/5½ oz plain flour
½ tsp baking powder
icing sugar, for dusting

1 Preheat the oven to 180°C/350°F/Gas Mark 4. Grease a 20 x 30-cm/8 x 12-inch rectangular cake tin and sprinkle with the breadcrumbs. Stone the cherries.

2 Put the butter and sugar into a large bowl and beat with an electric mixer until fluffy. Add the egg yolks, one at a time, beating after each addition until combined. Whisk the egg whites until they hold stiff peaks. Stir the almonds, flour and baking powder into the butter mixture, then fold in the beaten egg whites.

3 Spoon the mixture into the prepared tin and scatter the cherries on top.

4 Bake on the bottom shelf of the preheated oven for 50 minutes. At the end of the cooking time, switch off the oven and leave the cake inside for a further 10 minutes.

5 Remove from the oven and leave to cool in the tin. Turn out of the tin, dust with icing sugar and serve.

Apple and Cider Tart

Makes 1 tart 26 cm/10½ inches

Preparation time: 45 minutes,
   plus cooling
Cooking time: 35 minutes

Pastry
*300 g/10½ oz plain flour, plus extra
   for dusting*
1 tsp baking powder
*100 g/3½ oz butter, plus extra for
   greasing*
*150 g/5½ oz low-fat curd cheese
   or quark*
100 ml/3½ fl oz milk
80 g/2¾ oz caster sugar
1 tsp vanilla sugar (see page 10)
pinch of salt

Filling
*1 sachet vanilla blancmange
   powder*
2 eggs, separated
350 ml/12 fl oz milk
100 g/3½ oz caster sugar
150 ml/5 fl oz cider
pinch of salt
*750 g/1 lb 10 oz Golden Delicious
   apples*
juice of ½ lemon
whipped cream, to serve (optional)

1 Preheat the oven to 180°C/350°F/Gas Mark 4. Grease a
26-cm/10½-inch round tart tin.

2 To make the pastry, sift together the flour and the baking powder.
Melt the butter in a saucepan. Put the flour mixture into the bowl of
a food mixer with the curd cheese, milk, butter, caster sugar, vanilla
sugar and salt and mix to a smooth dough. Roll out the pastry on a
work surface lightly dusted with flour to a round slightly larger than
the tin. Line the prepared tin with the pastry, turning up the edge.

3 To make the filling, mix the blancmange powder with the egg
yolks and 4 tablespoons of the milk. Pour the remaining milk into
a saucepan with 80 g/2¾ oz of the sugar and bring to the boil. Pour
in the blancmange powder mixture, stirring, and bring back to the
boil. Add the cider and bring back to the boil. Transfer the mixture
to a bowl, cover with clingfilm and leave to cool in the refrigerator
until lukewarm.

4 Meanwhile, whisk the egg whites with the salt until they hold stiff
peaks, then fold into the lukewarm blancmange mixture. Spread the
mixture over the pastry and level the surface.

5 Peel, core and quarter the apples and cut them into thin slices.
Mix the apple slices with the remaining sugar and the lemon juice,
then arrange on top of the blancmange mixture in a circular pattern.

6 Bake in the preheated oven for about 35 minutes until golden
yellow. Leave to cool before serving with whipped cream, if using.

American Apple Pies

Makes 4 small pies

Preparation time: 1 hour, plus
   30 minutes to chill
Cooking time: 45–50 minutes

170 g/6 oz cold butter, plus extra
   for greasing
300 g/10½ oz plain flour, plus extra
   for dusting
pinch of salt
1 kg/2 lb 4 oz apples
150 g/5½ oz caster sugar
pinch of nutmeg
½ tsp ground cinnamon
grated rind of 1 lemon
1 egg yolk
3½ tbsp whipping cream
vanilla ice cream, to serve

1 To make the pastry, cut 130 g/4½ oz of the butter into small pieces. Put 280 g/10 oz of the flour, the salt and the pieces of butter into a food processor and process until a crumbly dough forms. Gradually add a few tablespoonfuls of very cold water and continue to process until the dough forms a ball. Wrap the dough in clingfilm and chill in the refrigerator for about 30 minutes.

2 Preheat the oven to 200°C/400°F/Gas Mark 6. Grease four 10-cm/4-inch tartlet tins.

3 To make the filling, peel and core the apples and cut into slices. Mix the apple slices with the sugar, nutmeg, cinnamon, lemon rind and the remaining flour.

4 Roll out two thirds of the pastry on a work surface lightly dusted with flour to a thickness of 3 mm/⅛ inch and use to line the prepared tins. Prick the bases with a fork in several places. Divide the apple mixture between the tins and dot with the remaining butter.

5 Roll out a third of the remaining pastry and cut into strips. Thinly roll out the remaining pastry to make four pastry lids and place these on top of the filling, sealing well around the edges. Pierce a few holes in the pastry lids. Beat together the egg yolk and the cream. Lay the pastry strips on top of the lids in a criss-cross pattern and brush with the egg yolk and cream mixture.

6 Bake in the preheated oven for about 45–50 minutes. Serve lukewarm with vanilla ice cream, or cold.

Cinnamon, Apple and Almond Cake

Makes 1 cake 24 cm/9½ inches

Preparation time: 45 minutes
Cooking time: 45 minutes

Cake
400 g/14 oz plain flour, plus extra
    for dusting
2 tsp baking powder
250 g/9 oz butter, plus extra for
    greasing
125 g/4½ oz caster sugar
4 eggs
pinch of salt
100 ml/3½ fl oz milk

Topping
1 kg/2 lb 4 oz apples
juice of ½ lemon
½ tsp ground cinnamon
50 g/1¾ oz caster sugar
85 g/3 oz flaked almonds
icing sugar, for dusting

1 Preheat the oven to 180°C/350°F/Gas Mark 4. Grease a 24-cm/ 9½-inch round springform tin and dust with flour.

2 To make the cake, sift together the flour and the baking powder. Put the butter into a large bowl and beat with an electric mixer until fluffy, gradually beating in the sugar, eggs, salt and flour mixture. Add the milk, a little at a time, beating after each addition until smooth.

3 Spoon the mixture into the prepared tin and level the surface with a palette knife.

4 To make the topping, peel, quarter and core the apples. Cut the quarters into thin slices and drizzle with the lemon juice. Dust the apple slices with the cinnamon and mix with the sugar and almonds.

5 Spread the apple mixture evenly on top of the cake mixture. Bake in the preheated oven for about 45 minutes. Remove from the oven and leave to cool. Unclip and release the springform, transfer the cake to a cake plate, dust with icing sugar and serve.

Apple and Cinnamon Cake

Makes 1 cake 28 cm/11 inches

Preparation time: 45 minutes
Cooking time: 30 minutes

Cake
150 g/5½ oz plain flour
75 g/2¾ oz cornflour
2 tsp baking powder
150 g/5½ oz softened butter, plus
  extra for greasing
125 g/4½ oz caster sugar
1 tsp icing sugar
4 eggs

Topping
750 g/1 lb 10 oz apples
40 g/1½ oz caster sugar
1 tsp ground cinnamon

1 Preheat the oven to 180°C/350°F/Gas Mark 4. Grease a 28-cm/11-inch tart dish or tin.

2 To make the cake, sift together the flour, cornflour and baking powder. Put the butter into a large bowl and beat with an electric mixer until fluffy. Gradually add the caster sugar and icing sugar, then add the eggs, one at a time, beating after each addition until combined. Add the flour mixture in two batches and mix to combine.

3 Spoon the mixture into the prepared tin and level the surface.

4 To make the topping, peel and core the apples and cut them into thin slices. Mix the apple slices with the sugar and cinnamon. Scatter the apple slices evenly over the mixture.

5 Bake in the preheated oven for about 30 minutes until lightly browned. Leave to cool in the dish, then cut into wedges and serve.

Grape and Soured Cream Flan

Makes 1 flan 26 cm/10½ inches

Preparation time: 40 minutes,
  plus cooling
Cooking time: 50 minutes

Pastry
butter, for greasing
270 g/9½ oz plain flour, plus extra
  for dusting
1 tsp baking powder
150 g/5½ oz low-fat curd cheese
  or quark
3½ tbsp milk
3½ tbsp vegetable oil
80 g/2¾ oz caster sugar
1 tsp vanilla sugar (see page 10)
pinch of salt

Filling
250 ml/9 fl oz soured cream
2 egg yolks
400 ml/14 fl oz milk
1 sachet vanilla blancmange
  powder
1 tsp vanilla sugar
60 g/2¼ oz caster sugar
350 g/12 oz mixed red and white
  grapes

1 Preheat the oven to 180°C/350°F/Gas Mark 4. Grease a 26-cm/10½-inch flan tin and line with baking paper.

2 To make the pastry, sift together the flour and the baking powder. Put the mixture into the bowl of a food mixer with the curd cheese, milk, oil, caster sugar, vanilla sugar and salt and work to a smooth dough using the dough hook.

3 Turn out the pastry onto a work surface lightly dusted with flour and roll out to 26-cm/10½-inch round, then place it in the prepared tin, turning it up at the edge.

4 To make the filling, mix the soured cream with the egg yolks. Mix 100 ml/3½ fl oz of the milk with the blancmange powder. Pour the remaining milk into a saucepan and add the vanilla sugar and caster sugar, then bring to the boil. Stir the blancmange mixture into the pan and bring to the boil. Remove from the heat and stir the blancmange mixture into the soured cream mixture. Leave to cool slightly.

5 Spread the cream filling over the pastry base. Arrange the grapes on top of the cream filling.

6 Bake in the preheated oven for about 50 minutes. After 30 minutes, cover with foil. Leave to cool completely before serving.

Tip: To make a glaze, bring 250 ml/9 fl oz white grape juice to the boil in a saucepan with 30 g/1 oz caster sugar. Add three sheets of soaked and squeezed leaf gelatine and leave to dissolve. Leave to cool until it starts to set. Pour over the cake and leave to stand until the glaze is fully set.

Banana and Chocolate Flan

Makes 1 flan 28 cm/11 inches

Preparation time: 55 minutes, plus 3 hours to chill

Base
150 g/5½ oz plain chocolate
20 g/¾ oz butter
150 g/5½ oz chocolate puffed rice cereal

Topping
600 g/1 lb 5 oz low-fat curd cheese or quark
100 g/3½ oz caster sugar
1 tsp vanilla sugar (see page 10)
grated rind of 1 lemon
3 ripe bananas, around 350 g/12 oz (peeled weight)
2 tbsp lemon juice
10 sheets leaf gelatine
200 ml/7 fl oz whipping cream
250 g/9 oz plain chocolate shavings

1 To make the base, break the chocolate into pieces, put it into a heatproof bowl set over a saucepan of gently simmering water, add the butter and heat until melted, stirring constantly. Whizz the cereal in a food processor and stir into the chocolate mixture.

2 Line a 28-cm/11-inch round springform tin with baking paper. Spoon the chocolate mixture into the prepared tin, pressing down well with the back of the spoon. Leave to chill in the refrigerator for 1 hour.

3 To make the topping, mix together the curd cheese, caster sugar, vanilla sugar and lemon rind in a bowl. Thinly slice the bananas and drizzle with the lemon juice. Soak the gelatine in cold water for 10 minutes, then gently squeeze out the water. Put the gelatine into a saucepan with a little water and stir over a medium heat until dissolved. Add the bananas and gelatine to the curd cheese mixture.

4 Whip the cream until it holds soft peaks, then use a spatula to fold it into the setting curd cheese and banana mixture. Spread the mixture over the base and level the surface with a palette knife. Leave to chill in the refrigerator for 2 hours.

5 Sprinkle the chocolate shavings over the flan. Unclip and release the springform, transfer the flan to a cake plate and serve.

Pineapple and Coconut Cake

Makes 1 cake 28 cm/11 inches

Preparation time: 50 minutes
Cooking time: 1 hour 20 minutes

Cake
*500 g/1 lb 2 oz freshly grated
coconut
400 ml/14 fl oz coconut milk
4 eggs, separated
300 g/10½ oz soft light brown sugar
200 g/7 oz plain flour
80 g/2¾ oz cornflour
2 tsp baking powder
½ tsp ground cardamom
½ tsp ground cinnamon
120 g/4¼ oz ground almonds*

Topping
*½ pineapple
150 g/5½ oz ginger jam
30 g/1 oz freshly grated coconut*

1 Preheat the oven to 160°C/325°F/Gas Mark 3. Line a 28-cm/11-inch round springform tin with baking paper.

2 To make the topping, peel and quarter the pineapple and cut out the hard centre. Cut the quarters into 3-mm/⅛-inch thick slices and set aside until required.

3 To make the cake, put the coconut into a blender with the coconut milk in batches and whizz until the coconut is finely ground. Transfer the coconut mixture to a bowl.

4 Put the egg yolks into a bowl with half the sugar and beat with an electric mixer until fluffy. Add the coconut mixture and mix to combine. Mix together the flour, cornflour, baking powder, cardamom, cinnamon and almonds. Stir the flour mixture into the coconut mixture. Put the egg whites into a separate bowl and whisk until they hold stiff peaks, adding the remaining sugar a little at a time. Carefully fold into the coconut mixture.

5 Spoon the mixture into the prepared tin and arrange the pineapple slices on top in a fan arrangement. Bake in the preheated oven for about 80 minutes until golden brown. Leave to cool slightly, then remove from the tin and transfer to a wire rack to cool completely.

6 Heat the jam in a saucepan over a low heat, then pass it through a sieve and use to brush the top of the cake. Scatter over the grated coconut just before serving.

Tip: Fresh coconut slices are often available in the fresh fruit section of supermarkets. Alternatively, pour 200 ml/7 fl oz hot water over 300 g/10½ oz desiccated coconut and leave to soak for 10 minutes.

Pomegranate Cheesecake

Makes 1 cheesecake 24 cm/
9½ inches

Preparation time: 30 minutes, plus
4½ hours to chill

Base
225 g/8 oz sweet oat biscuits
75 g/2¾ oz butter, plus extra for
greasing

Filling
9 sheets leaf gelatine
500 g/1 lb 2 oz low-fat curd cheese
or quark
3 tbsp orange juice
75 g/2¾ oz icing sugar
200 ml/7 fl oz whipping cream
2 egg whites

Topping
2 sheets leaf gelatine
100 ml/3½ fl oz pomegranate juice
3 tbsp kirsch
40 g/1½ oz caster sugar
2 pomegranates, seeds scraped out

1 Grease a 24-cm/9½-inch round springform tin. Put the biscuits into a polythene bag and crush with a rolling pin until reduced to fine crumbs. Melt the butter in a saucepan, add the biscuit crumbs and mix well. Press the mixture into the base of the prepared tin, then chill in the refrigerator for 30 minutes.

2 To make the filling, soak the gelatine in cold water for 10 minutes. Mix together the curd cheese, orange juice and icing sugar in a large bowl and gradually stir in the cream. Put the egg whites into a separate bowl and whisk until they hold stiff peaks. Gently squeeze the water out of the gelatine. Put the gelatine into a saucepan over a medium heat and stir until dissolved. Stir the gelatine into the curd cheese mixture and carefully fold in the egg whites.

3 Pour the filling into the tin, level the surface, cover with clingfilm and chill in the refrigerator for 2 hours.

4 Meanwhile, to make the topping, soak the gelatine in cold water for 10 minutes. Put the pomegranate juice into a saucepan with the kirsch and sugar and bring to the boil. Gently squeeze the water out of the gelatine and dissolve the gelatine in the pomegranate juice mixture. Remove from the heat, add the pomegranate seeds and leave to cool.

5 Spread the pomegranate jelly over the set cheesecake and chill for 2 hours. Remove the cake from the tin and transfer to a cake plate to serve.

Yeast Cake with Mango

Makes 1 cake 30 × 40 cm/
  12 × 16 inches

Preparation time: 35 minutes, plus
  approx 30 minutes to rise
Cooking time: 40-45 minutes

Cake
450 g/1 lb plain flour, plus extra
  for dusting
80 g/2¾ oz caster sugar
pinch of salt
1 x 7 g sachet easy-blend dried
  yeast
200 ml/7 fl oz lukewarm milk
grated rind of ½ lemon
2 eggs, beaten
80 g/2½ oz softened butter, plus
  extra for greasing

Topping
2 ripe mangos
30 g/1 oz softened butter
1 egg, separated
50 g/1¾ oz brown sugar
125 g/4½ oz low-fat curd cheese or
  quark
20 g/¾ oz plain flour
grated rind of ½ lemon
pinch of salt
2 egg yolks, beaten
20 g/¾ oz desiccated coconut

1 To make the cake, sift the flour, sugar and salt into a large bowl then stir in the yeast. Make a well in the centre.

2 Add the milk, lemon rind, eggs and butter to the dry ingredients and knead to a very soft dough. Cover with a damp tea towel and leave to rise in a warm place for about 30 minutes, until risen and springy to the touch.

3 Preheat the oven to 180°C/350°F/Gas Mark 4. Grease a 30 x 40-cm/12 x 16-inch baking tray.

4 To make the topping, peel the mangos, cut the flesh away from the stones and cut into thin slices. Put the butter into a bowl and beat with an electric mixer until fluffy. Add the egg yolk and sugar, a little at a time, beating after each addition until combined. Mix in the curd cheese, flour and lemon rind. Whisk the egg white with the salt in a separate bowl until it holds stiff peaks, then fold into the curd cheese mixture.

5 Turn out the dough onto a work surface dusted with flour and roll out to a 30 x 40-cm/12 x 16-inch rectangle. Lay it in the prepared tray, spread the curd cheese mixture evenly over the dough and arrange the mango slices on top.

6 Brush the cake with the beaten egg yolk and bake in the preheated oven for about 45 minutes until golden brown. Leave to cool, then sprinkle with the coconut and serve.

Chilled Buttermilk and Kiwi Fruit Flan

Makes 1 flan 28 cm/11 inches

Preparation time: 35 minutes, plus
  3 hours to chill
Cooking time: 25 minutes

Choux pastry
250 ml/9 fl oz water
60 g/2¼ oz butter
pinch of salt
30 g/1 oz caster sugar
150 g/5½ oz plain flour
3 eggs

Filling
14 sheets leaf gelatine
1 litre/1¾ pints buttermilk
juice of 2 lemons
100 g/3½ oz caster sugar
2 tsp vanilla sugar (see page 10)
200 ml/7 fl oz whipping cream
4 large kiwi fruit, peeled and sliced

1 Preheat the oven to 220°C/425°F/Gas Mark 7. Line a large baking sheet with baking paper.

2 To make the choux pastry, put the water, butter, salt and sugar into a saucepan and bring to the boil. Add the flour and stir vigorously with a wooden spoon until the mixture comes away from the base of the pan in a lump, leaving a white film. Remove from the heat and add the eggs, one at a time, beating with an electric mixer after each addition until combined.

3 Put the dough into a piping bag fitted with a medium tip and pipe onto the prepared baking sheet from a distance of 1 cm/½ inch to make a spiral with a diameter of 28 cm/11 inches. Pipe any remaining dough in strips next to the spiral. Place the baking sheet on the middle shelf of the preheated oven and pour a small cup of water onto the floor of the oven. Bake for 25 minutes until golden brown. Remove from the oven and transfer to a wire rack to cool.

4 To make the filling, soak the gelatine in cold water for about 10 minutes. Mix together the buttermilk, lemon juice, caster sugar and vanilla sugar. Squeeze the water out of the gelatine, put the gelatine into a saucepan with a little water, and heat over a low heat, stirring constantly, until dissolved. Stir into the buttermilk mixture. Chill the mixture until it starts to set. Whip the cream until it holds stiff peaks and fold into the buttermilk mixture in two batches.

5 Clip a 28-cm/11-inch round springform ring around the choux pastry spiral. Pour in the filling and spread evenly. Chill for 3 hours.

6 Break the baked strips of pastry into pieces. Arrange the kiwi fruit on top of the flan and sprinkle with the pastry pieces. Unclip and release the springform and transfer the flan to a serving plate.

Mandarin Cheesecake

Makes 1 cheesecake 22 cm/
  8½ inches

Preparation time: 30 minutes,
  plus 3½ hours to chill

Base
150 g/5½ oz sponge fingers
125 g/4½ oz butter

Filling
800 g/1 lb 12 oz canned mandarin
  segments
600 g/1 lb 5 oz cream cheese
350 ml/12fl oz natural yogurt
3 tbsp orange juice
150 ml/5 fl oz Italian aperitif, such
  as Campari®
10 sheets leaf gelatine
100 g/3½ oz caster sugar

1 Line the base of a 22-cm/8½-inch round springform tin with baking paper and close the springform around it.

2 To make the base, put the sponge fingers into a polythene bag and crush with a rolling pin until reduced to fine crumbs. Reserve 2 tablespoons for the decoration. Melt the butter in a saucepan, pour it over the remaining crumbs and mix until combined. Spoon the mixture into the prepared tin, spreading it over the base and pressing down firmly. Chill in the refrigerator for 30 minutes.

3 To make the filling, carefully drain the mandarin segments, reserving half the juice. Put the cream cheese into a food processor with the yogurt, orange juice and aperitif and whizz until smooth.

4 Soak the gelatine in cold water for about 10 minutes. Put the sugar and the reserved juice into a saucepan and bring to the boil. Squeeze the water out of the gelatine, then add the gelatine to the pan and heat, stirring constantly, until dissolved. Remove from the heat and leave to stand until it is beginning to set.

5 Gradually mix the gelatine mixture into the cream cheese mixture. Carefully mix in half the mandarin segments and spoon the mixture into the tin. Level the surface, cover with clingfilm and chill in the refrigerator for 3 hours.

6 Remove the clingfilm and unclip and release the springform. Arrange the remaining mandarin segments on top of the cake and sprinkle the reserved crumbs on top.

Tip: The cheesecake can be made with fresh strawberries in summer. It can also be made with canned peach slices if mandarin segments are not available.

Angela's Orange Tart

Makes 1 tart 24 cm/9½ inches

Preparation time: 35 minutes, plus
  1 hour to chill
Cooking time: 1 hour 5 minutes

Pastry
150 g/5½ oz butter, diced, plus
  extra for greasing
250 g/9 oz plain flour, plus extra
  for dusting
40 g/1½ oz caster sugar
pinch of salt
1 egg
grated rind of ½ orange
2 tbsp lukewarm water

Filling
1 egg
3 egg yolks
120 g/4¼ oz caster sugar
400 ml/14 fl oz crème fraîche
grated rind and juice of 1 orange
3 tbsp orange marmalade
strips of orange zest, for decorating

1 To make the pastry, put the butter, flour, sugar, salt, egg, orange rind and water into a large bowl and knead until a soft dough forms. Wrap the pastry in clingfilm and chill in the refrigerator for at least 1 hour.

2 Preheat the oven to 180°C/350°F/Gas Mark 4. Grease a 24-cm/9½-inch fluted tart tin.

3 To make the filling, put the egg, egg yolks and sugar into a bowl and beat with an electric mixer until fluffy. Put the crème fraîche into a saucepan and heat over a low heat, whisking constantly with a balloon whisk. Mix in the orange rind and juice.

4 Add the hot orange mixture to the egg mixture and mix well. Pass through a fine sieve into a bowl and leave to cool.

5 Roll out the pastry on a work surface dusted with flour to a thickness of 3 mm/⅛ inch. Use to line the prepared tin, trimming any surplus with a knife. Prick the base with a fork in several places.

6 Line with baking paper, fill with baking beans and bake blind on the bottom shelf of the preheated oven for 15 minutes. Remove the beans and paper and bake for a further 15 minutes. Remove from the oven and reduce the oven temperature to 160°C/325°F/Gas Mark 3.

7 Brush the base of the pastry case with the marmalade. Pour the orange mixture into the hot pastry case and bake for a further 35 minutes. Remove from the oven and leave to cool. Sprinkle over the orange zest just before serving.

Lemon Sponge Roll

Makes 1 roll 40cm/16 inches

Preparation time: 50 minutes, plus
   5 hours to cool and chill
Cooking time: 20 minutes

Sponge
5 eggs, separated
4 tbsp lukewarm water
75 g/2¾ oz caster sugar
90 g/3¼ oz plain flour
55 g/2 oz cornflour
1 tsp baking powder

Filling
juice of 3 lemons
grated rind of 1 lemon
60 g/2¼ oz caster sugar
350 ml/12 fl oz water
5 sheets leaf gelatine
250 ml/9 fl oz whipping cream
icing sugar, for dusting
150 g/5½ oz blueberries,
  to decorate

1 Preheat the oven to 170°C/325°F/Gas Mark 3. Line a 30 × 40-cm/12 × 16-inch baking tray with baking paper.

2 To make the sponge, put the egg whites into a large bowl with the water and whisk until they hold stiff peaks. Gradually add the sugar, stirring constantly, until combined. Beat the egg yolks and carefully fold in. Sift together the flour, cornflour and baking powder into the egg mixture and fold in carefully.

3 Spread the mixture evenly in the prepared tray and bake on the middle shelf of the preheated oven for about 20 minutes.

4 Remove from the oven and immediately invert onto a damp tea towel. Brush the baking paper with cold water and peel off quickly. Use the tea towel to roll up the sponge, from the long side, then leave to cool for 2 hours.

5 To make the filling, put the lemon juice, lemon rind, sugar and water into a saucepan, bring to the boil, boil briefly, then remove from the heat. Soak the gelatine in a little cold water for 10 minutes, then squeeze out the water. Stir the gelatine into the warm lemon syrup and leave to cool.

6 Whip the cream until it holds stiff peaks. As soon as the lemon mixture begins to set, fold in the cream.

7 Carefully unroll the sponge and spread with the lemon cream. Roll up again immediately and chill in the refrigerator for 3 hours.

8 Just before serving, dust the roll with the icing sugar, cut into slices and decorate with the blueberries.

Angela's Lemon Tart

Makes 1 tart 24 cm/9½ inches

Preparation time: 25 minutes,
  plus 30 minutes to chill
Cooking time: 1 hour 5 minutes

Pastry
*200 g/7 oz plain flour, plus extra
  for dusting
90 g/3¼ oz icing sugar
90 g/3¼ oz ground almonds
140 g/5 oz butter, plus extra
  for greasing
1 egg
pinch of salt*

Filling
*grated rind and juice of 3 lemons
150 g/5½ oz butter
265 g/9½ oz caster sugar
4 eggs*

Topping
*2 lemons, thinly sliced
100 ml/3½ fl oz water
100 g/3½ oz caster sugar*

1 To make the pastry, mix together the flour, icing sugar and almonds. Melt the butter in a saucepan. Combine the flour mixture with the butter, egg and salt in a food processer, then knead by hand until a smooth dough forms, wrap in clingfilm and chill in the refrigerator for 30 minutes.

2 Preheat the oven to 180°C/350°F/Gas Mark 4. Grease a 24-cm/9½-inch round tart tin.

3 To make the filling, put the lemon rind and juice, butter and sugar into a saucepan over a low heat and heat, stirring constantly, until the sugar has dissolved. Whisk the eggs with a balloon whisk until frothy, then add them to the lemon mixture. Remove from the heat and continue stirring until smooth and creamy.

4 Roll out the dough on a work surface lightly dusted with flour into a 5-mm/¼-inch thick round. Lay it in the flan tin, pressing it into place and trimming off any surplus with a sharp knife. Prick the base with a fork in several places.

5 Line with baking paper, fill with baking beans and bake on the bottom shelf of the preheated oven for 15 minutes. Remove the beans and paper and bake for a further 15 minutes. Remove from the oven and reduce the oven temperature to 140°C/275°F/Gas Mark 1. Pour the filling into the pastry case and bake for a further 35 minutes. Transfer to a wire rack to cool.

6 Meanwhile, to make the topping, put the lemon slices into a shallow saucepan, add the water and sugar, bring to the boil and simmer for 10 minutes. Remove from the heat and leave to cool.

7 Arrange the lemon slices on top of the tart and serve.

Fig and Orange Liqueur Cake

Makes 1 cake 24 cm/9½ inches

Preparation time: 40 minutes
Cooking time: 40 minutes

Cake
70 g/2½ oz dried figs
120 g/4¼ oz butter, plus extra
  for greasing
½ vanilla pod
4 eggs, separated
150 g/5½ oz caster sugar
3 tbsp cornflour
225 g/8 oz ground almonds
4 tsp orange liqueur

Topping
400 g/14 oz fresh figs
200 ml/7 fl oz whipping cream
50 g/1¾ oz icing sugar, plus extra
  for dusting
20 g/¾ oz toasted flaked almonds,
  for sprinkling

1 Preheat the oven to 200°C/400°F/Gas Mark 6. Grease a 24-cm/9½-inch round springform tin.

2 To make the cake, finely chop the figs. Melt the butter in a small saucepan. Halve the vanilla pod lengthways and scrape out the seeds.

3 Put the egg yolks into a bowl with 100 g/3½ oz of the sugar and the vanilla seeds and beat with an electric mixer until fluffy. Add the cornflour, figs, almonds, melted butter and liqueur and mix to combine.

4 Whisk the egg whites in a separate bowl until they hold soft peaks. Add the remaining sugar, a little at a time, whisking until the egg white holds stiff peaks. Carefully fold into the fig mixture.

5 Spoon the mixture into the prepared tin and bake on the middle shelf of the preheated oven for 40 minutes. Remove from the oven and leave to cool completely. Unclip and release the springform and transfer the cake to a cake plate.

6 To make the topping, halve the figs. Put the cream into a bowl, add the icing sugar and whip until it holds stiff peaks. Spread the cream on top of the cake and arrange the figs on top of the cream. Sprinkle over the almonds and dust with icing sugar.

Tip: Arrange some fig leaves on the plate and lay the cake on top of them to serve.

Sherry Trifle
with Tipsy Fruit

Makes 8 small trifles

Preparation time: 45 minutes,
  plus time to stand

1 sachet vanilla blancmange
  powder
500 ml/18 fl oz milk
250 g/9 oz sponge fingers
100 g/3½ oz apricot jam
200 ml/7 fl oz dry sherry
2 oranges
2 nectarines
1 ripe banana
1 vanilla pod
200 ml/7 fl oz whipping cream
40 g/1½ oz caster sugar

1 Prepare the vanilla blancmange with the milk according to the packet instructions, pour into a bowl, cover with clingfilm and leave to cool for 1 hour.

2 Crush the sponge fingers into chunks and place in a shallow bowl. Mix the jam with 150 ml/5 fl oz of the sherry, carefully mix with the sponge finger pieces, cover with clingfilm and set aside.

3 Cut off a 1-cm/½-inch slice from the top and bottom of each orange. Peel the oranges, removing both the outer skin and the white pith. Cut with a small knife inside the membrane of each orange segment and separate the flesh from the membranes. Collect any orange juice in a bowl.

4 Halve and stone the nectarines and cut into small pieces. Cut the banana in half lengthways, then cut into thin slices. Mix with the orange segments and nectarine pieces. Pour the remaining sherry over the top and leave to soak for 30 minutes.

5 Divide the sponge finger mixture among 8 glass dishes and spoon over the fruit and orange juice, reserving some fruit to decorate.

6 Halve the vanilla pod lengthways and scrape out the seeds. Whip the cream with the vanilla seeds and sugar until it holds stiff peaks. Beat the blancmange with a balloon whisk until smooth, then fold in the cream.

7 Spoon the cream mixture into the dishes and tap the dishes on the work surface to allow the mixture to settle. Decorate with the remaining fruit pieces and serve chilled.

Tamarillo Cake with Chocolate

Makes 1 cake 24 cm/9½ inches

Preparation time: 45 minutes,
  plus 4 hours to chill
Cooking time: 50 minutes

Cake
butter, for greasing
5 eggs, separated
pinch of salt
3 tbsp water
150 g/5½ oz caster sugar
100 g/3½ oz plain flour
20 g/¾ oz cornflour
40 g/1½ oz cocoa powder

Filling
2 tamarillos
8 sheets leaf gelatine
3 tbsp orange liqueur
110 g/3¾ oz icing sugar
500 ml/18 fl oz whipping cream
2 tsp vanilla sugar (see page 10)

Topping
2 tamarillos
100 g/3½ oz quince jelly

Note
*If you can't find tamarillos, use
  ripe Sharon fruit instead.*

1 Preheat the oven to 180°C/350°F/Gas Mark 4. Grease a 24-cm/9½-inch round springform tin.

2 Put the egg whites into a bowl with the salt and whisk until they hold stiff peaks. Beat the egg yolks with the water and sugar until the sugar has dissolved. Mix the flour with the cornflour and cocoa powder and loosely fold into the egg yolk mixture with the egg whites.

3 Spoon the mixture into the prepared tin. Bake in the preheated oven for 50 minutes, then turn out onto a wire rack and leave to cool.

4 To make the filling, peel the tamarillos with a vegetable peeler, remove the stalks and purée the fruit using a hand-held blender. Soak the gelatine in cold water for about 10 minutes, then squeeze out and place it in a small saucepan with the liqueur and heat over a low heat until dissolved. Mix with the tamarillo purée and icing sugar.

5 Whip the cream with the vanilla sugar until it holds stiff peaks. Fold the tamarillo mixture into the cream.

6 Halve the sponge horizontally. Replace the bottom half in the tin and spread the tamarillo cream on top. Place the other half on top, cover the tin with clingfilm and leave to set in the refrigerator for about 4 hours.

7 To make the topping, peel the tamarillos with a vegetable peeler, remove the stalks and cut the fruit into thin slices with a sharp knife. Arrange the slices on the cake in a circular pattern. Put the jelly into a small saucepan and heat over a low heat, then brush it over the tamarillo slices.

Index

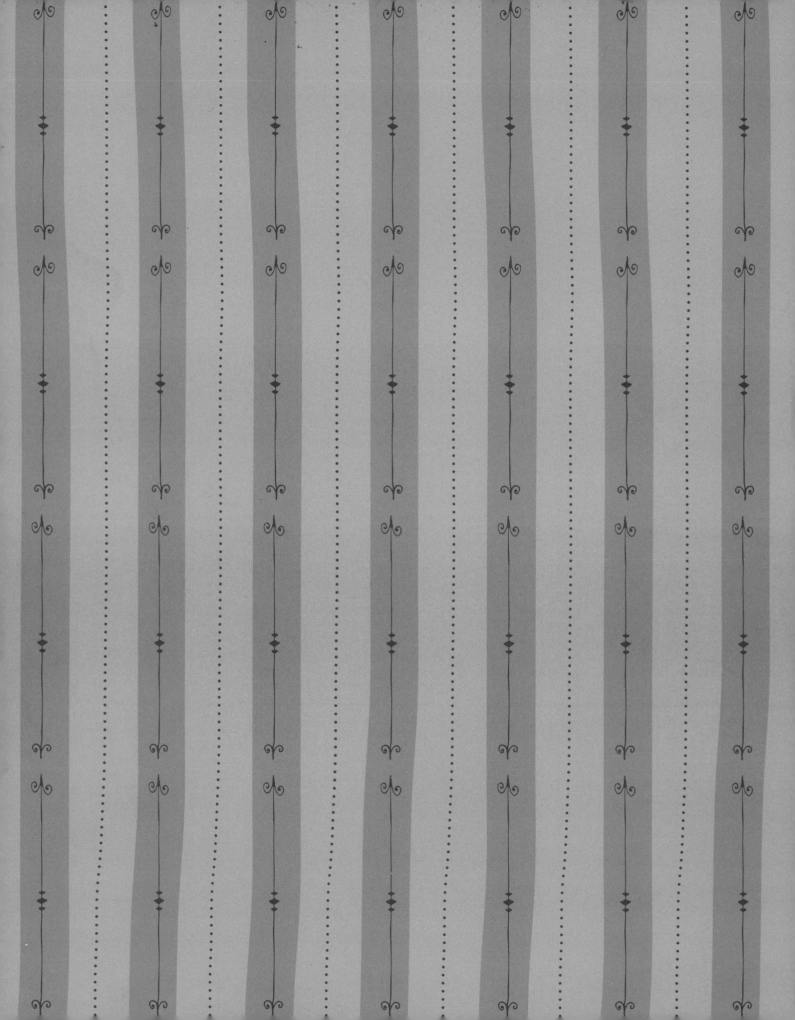